Philippine Duchesne
A Global View

Philippine Duchesne
A Global View

Edited by

Kathleen Hughes, RSCJ

Society of the Sacred Heart

Saint Louis, Missouri

Philippine Duchesne, A Global View
Edited byKathleen Hughes, RSCJ

Book design by Peggy Nehmen, n-kcreative.com

Printed in the United States of America
ISBN-13: 978-0-9971329-6-0

Published by:

Society of the Sacred Heart™
United States – Canada

4120 Forest Park Avenue
St. Louis Missouri 63108-2809
314-652-1500
RSCJ.org

Contents

Introduction

Philippine Duchesne: A Global View gathers together the reflections of the worldwide community of Religious of the Sacred Heart (RSCJ) about one of their own, Saint Rose Philippine Duchesne. It celebrates the 200th anniversary of Philippine's journey to the New World, together with Eugénie Audé, Octavie Berthold, Catherine Lamarre, and Marguerite Manteau, five companions who came from France to the Louisiana Territory at the request of Bishop William Dubourg to begin their ministry on the frontier. Their arrival marked the beginning of Catholic education in what would become the Archdiocese of St. Louis, the establishment of Sacred Heart education in the Americas, and the point at which the Society of the Sacred Heart became an international community, now serving in more than forty countries. Truly, the impact of that perilous ocean journey in 1818 is extraordinary.

From this vantage point, it is easy to celebrate the success of their adventure without thinking too much about the cost. These women found themselves in a country, a culture, a set of social mores, a language, and a way of life that were totally bewildering. Physical conditions, especially compared to what they had known in France, were harsh. There was never enough of what they needed, either of personnel or finance, to keep up with the demands of their work or the growing number of people they wished to serve.

It was, for all of them in different ways, a very lonely existence, separated as they were from the world they had left behind: their families, familiar spiritual supports, and the larger community that had nourished their vocations and then sent them, with blessings, to this far field.

Certainly this loneliness was felt most keenly by Philippine because of her friendship with Saint Madeleine Sophie Barat, the founder of the Society of the Sacred Heart and Philippine's mentor, confidante, and life-long friend. In our day of instant communication, it is unfathomable that the response to a letter might be half a year later – or might never arrive because of the vagaries of the post and of transportation in general. Meanwhile decisions had to be taken, communities founded, novices welcomed, classes and other tasks assigned, and monies raised to support the whole enterprise.

Philippine was the reluctant leader of this little band of missionaries, the Society of the Sacred Heart's public face to Church and state alike, the one among her companions who was the decision-maker in matters large and small. It was not a role she sought or felt competent to fulfill. Leadership was one more struggle in her life.

The bicentennial of Philippine's arrival in the New World in 1818 has been a time to learn more about this intrepid woman – not simply the saint we thought we knew, but the real flesh and blood woman. She was canonized by the Church not because she was perfect but because – in the midst of challenges of every kind and of her own conviction that she was a failure – she was a woman of profound prayer who joined herself to the Heart of Jesus Christ and modeled her life on his death for the life of the world.

To celebrate the internationality Philippine made possible, brief reflections about her were requested from all parts of the Society of the Sacred Heart. An international editorial committee was formed, including Religious of the Sacred Heart: Park Jeong Mi from Korea, Françoise Greffe from France, Elizabeth Nakayiza from Uganda, and Kimberly King from Canada. It was the role of this committee to solicit reflections about Philippine and her relevance for today from women living in their geographic region. Thirty-one countries are represented among the authors.

Thanks also are due to a final editorial committee: Kathleen Conan, RSCJ; Frances Gimber, RSCJ; Carolyn Osiek, RSCJ; Clare Pratt, RSCJ; and Catherine Swanstrom. This committee worked on all fifty-two submissions for accuracy and consistency. The General Secretariat of the Society of the Scared Heart provided excellent translations of all texts in English, French, and Spanish, the three official languages of the Society.

The images accompanying this collection of texts offer a wide-ranging view of Philippine's life: we see her pictured onboard ship, at prayer, with various children gathered around her, and with her beloved Potawatomi, the people who had touched and enflamed her missionary imagination. Other images were chosen by the writer to illustrate the meaning of the reflection or to provide something of the backstory of Philippine. Her name itself – Duchesne – means "of oak." Acorns, oak leaves, and trees appear with some regularity in these pages; so, too, do reflections about Philippine's strength and courage implied by the powerful oak. The *Rebecca*, the name of the ship that brought Philippine and her companions to the Americas, also inspired some writers to use images of nineteenth century ships. Others more often employ the name of the ship as a metaphor – sometimes referred to as "a Rebecca moment" – conjuring those times when we know the tug of a new invitation to venture into the deep, to cross frontiers, and to discover and nurture new life, however perilous the crossing may appear.

Perhaps most pervasive through these pages is the name the Potawatomi gave to Philippine – Quah-Kah-Ka-num-ad (Woman who prays always). This deeply contemplative quality of Philippine's life has been picked up by nearly all who have written, perhaps because the writers, all but one a Religious of the Sacred Heart, share the same call to give themselves completely to a life of prayer even as they are also wholly available to the particular ministry that is theirs. Philippine is a witness that such balance is possible and fruitful.

The essays in this collection reflect many facets of this woman who is our sister and our friend. They introduce Philippine to those who do not know her well and deepen the appreciation and affection of those who have long known her but may read here a side of the saint they had not considered. The subjects of these reflections are as varied as the background of the writers: friendship, suffering, loss, courage, boundaries, failure, perseverance, hope, mission.

The attentive reader will also pick up several themes that are woven throughout the collection. These themes spring from a meeting in the summer of 2016, a General Chapter convened by the Society of the Sacred Heart, composed of Religious of the Sacred Heart from around the world. One of the chief tasks of a Chapter is to give fresh orientation to the Society, being aware of the needs of the Church and the world, guided by the Gospel and the Society's Constitutions. Four orientations, or "Chapter Calls," emerged from Chapter 2016: to reach new frontiers, to live more humanly, to create silence, and to be and to act as one Body. All of these orientations are illustrated in Philippine's extraordinary life.

The bicentennial celebration of Saint Rose Philippine Duchesne has been a rich and varied experience throughout the Sacred Heart family, including a spirituality forum, an academic conference, a global service day, books, lesson plans, a Mass commissioned in her honor, a new sculpture, pilgrimages to sites of her life, and so on. But, surely, the most important part of our celebration worldwide has been the preparation and posting of the reflections now gathered in these pages, offering a way that the family of the Sacred Heart could be united in prayer week after week across the world in celebration of Philippine, inspired by her life and challenged by her choices.

The bicentennial has drawn to a close, but we hope these brief reflections will continue to shed light on this woman who has drawn us together in shared prayer worldwide. Let her spirit speak to you as you ponder these thoughts and, if so moved, as you jot down your own brief essay to capture who she is for you and what she stirs in your heart.

Kathleen Hughes, RSCJ
August 29, 2019
The 250th Anniversary of Philippine Duchesne's Birth

Image: Annett Hanrahan, RSCJ
Province of Australia-New Zealand

Prayer of the Potawatomi on Hearing of the Death of Philippine

Sharon Karam, RSCJ
Province of the United States-Canada

She comes, Great Spirit,
she comes soon.
Comfort her spirit and care for her passage.
Let the grasses of the fields whisper her homecoming.
Let the lapping of the Mississippi's water
change her back to you.
Put out your colors this morning in all four season's flowers.
Let them bloom all at once in her honor.
Let the mockingbird, known for cleverness,
imitate all manner of songs, one for each mood of our hearts.
For we are sad; she was our sister.
We are glad, too; she is your child.
We are sorry; too many miles prevent our putting out this blanket
once more, over her shoulders.
(She learned weaving from our hands;
we learned to pray from her face.)
Let the sun blaze forth her compassion,
and the full moon tonight remind us
of her hours praising you in this tent.
Our village will keep vigil tonight.
Chief declares a fast in her name until tomorrow.
We will pray in what was her tent
for both our peoples, and for all those places
on the flat map which she left for us.
Creator, hear our prayer for her, for our children,
for those prairies, trees, and rivers,
for the faraway mountains and this brook which holds our tears.
Hear our sighs for these, our children,
that they remember what she taught them
And recall her name, for many moons, as your great woman.

Image: Milton Frenzel

Waiting on God

Katie Mifsud, RSCJ
Community of Malta

Dear Philippine,

When I first met you I was impressed by your many qualities, which spoke deeply to my heart. Today I wish to reflect with you about your patient waiting, in faith and hope, to fulfil your dreams.

It began in 1792, when the monastery where you were a novice was confiscated, and you had to return home. Then followed years of waiting before joining the Society, going to America, and finally, in 1841, to the Potawatomi, too old and too sick to do anything but pray.

What message do you have for us today, Philippine? In our world of instant coffee, commmunication, gratification, even happiness, have we forgotten how to wait? To hope and pray? Have we forgotten how to follow a dream? To aim high?

What gave you the inspiration to continue knocking on the Lord's door, believing your prayer would be granted? Was it your intense prayer life? Your love of the Eucharist? How do we learn to discern whether the Lord is saying "no" or "yes, but not yet"? To "wait for God's time" and know when it arrives?

Only the poor know how to wait. Teach us that poverty of heart that knows it can do nothing of itself, is open to the will of the Lord and ready to wait for it to manifest itself. Teach us to have vision, to journey to new frontiers, to persevere in our dreams, to wait for their fulfilment. As you did. ◦୬

Image: Historical marker located south of Plymouth in Marshall County, Indiana
Fulton County Historical Society

What Drove Her to Prayer?

Sheila Smith, RSCJ
Province of the United States-Canada

In 1841 Philippine Duchesne arrived at a new frontier – St. Mary's Mission in Sugar Creek, Kansas. There she lived with people who today we would call internally displaced persons. The Potawatomi had not only been forcibly displaced from their traditional homeland in Indiana, but had suffered deaths and murders of family members by American militia along the Trail of Death. These events took place between 1838 and 1840, just before Philippine's arrival.

Like us, Philippine was shaped by her faith and by the social attitudes and political context of her day. The Trail of Death was a nineteenth century political action that forcibly changed the lives of the Potawatomi. It also influenced Philippine and her companions, whose intention was to join in the Church's mission of evangelization and to start a girls' school for the Potawatomi.

What did Philippine see when she arrived among the Potawatomi with whom she could not communicate? Did she feel their suffering from the brutality of forced displacement? If so, how did she integrate the politics of her day with the Society's mission of love and her faith in the Gospel? What did this deeply contemplative woman pray about during long hours while she lived among the Potawatomi? As we reach for new frontiers in our contemporary world, we too come shaped by the politics and attitudes of our day. For what do we pray? Are our social attitudes and political actions congruent with the Gospel values we profess? ❧

Image: Montée de Chalemont
leading up to the Monastery of Sainte-Marie d'En-Haut

Healing Love

Phil Kilroy, RSCJ
Province of Ireland-Scotland

In the spring of 1804, Sophie Barat was seriously ill, and doctors in Paris could only ease her condition, not cure it. A turning point came in July 1806, when Sophie spent some weeks in Grenoble with Philippine Duchesne. During this visit Philippine nursed Sophie back to health. Sophie's recovery took place only when she had left Grenoble, but she was sure it was due to Philippine's loving care.

On 1 August 1806, Sophie wrote to Philippine telling her how much their deepening friendship meant to her and how she had been healed:

You know the state I was in when I left you. I was still in Lyon when all symptoms had disappeared. All disappeared in a night. I am completely healed.

Sophie confirmed her complete cure on 30 August 1806, and told Philippine:

The Lord has blessed your good care of me. I have had no further symptoms of my illness since Lyon.

From 1818, Philippine and Sophie spent their lives apart, one in Europe and the other in Missouri. The healing energy of love between them would always exist, however long apart they were physically, however difficult and erratic their communications, however diverse and difficult their experiences. That energy, that love, could cross and re-cross the Atlantic waves and reach their shores. And they were sure of it, they could count on it, and they did, to the end.

Image of Philippine: Milton Frenzel
Image of landscape: Rita Carroll, RSCJ, Province of Australia-New Zealand

Pools of Silence in This Thirsty Land*

Geneviève Bannon, RSCJ
Province of Australia-New Zealand

There is much in Philippine's life of prayer that could be a source of reflection for us, but today let us focus on just one aspect – how her prayer touched and inspired others, especially her beloved Potawatomi.

Philippine is nearing the end of her life after physical illness and much heart suffering. She is at last at Sugar Creek among the Potawatomi peoples to whom she longed to bring knowledge of the Heart of Jesus. She is unable to learn their language, but they have observed her at prayer and felt her kindness and her concern for them. As is their custom, they have given her a name expressive of who she essentially is, Quah-Kah-Ka-num-ad (woman-who-prays-always).

Philippine is important to them in herself, but she is also a signpost pointing beyond herself to the Great Spirit, the Native American name for God. It is the Great Spirit who gives her life meaning, inspiration, beauty and love. Through Philippine the Great Spirit calls the Potawatomi to find new meaning for their own lives – new inspiration, beauty and love.

Today, Philippine's example invites each of us to live and pray in such a way that others, especially the young, may see new possibilities in their own lives and so choose what is truly life-giving. ⮞

*Title and photograph inspired by the Australian poet, James McCauley, who likens prayer to "pools of silence in this thirsty land."

Image: Mary Beth Kemper, CPPS

Heart to Heart for Hearts

Elizabeth Kasyoka, RSCJ
Province of Uganda-Kenya

Ever since I have come to know Saint Philippine, she has become my friend and companion on my spiritual journey. Philippine's voyage to the New World resulted from a profound conversation and call from the Heart to her heart for all hearts. God beckoned her to let go, take action and move, to trust in the winds that would pelt the sails of her *Rebecca*, and to hold onto the rudder tightly and courageously on the high seas.

Philippine faced many setbacks, though they did not alter her dream of reaching the hearts she longed to touch. She was an educator and loved children. Not able to speak the language of the people, she spoke with her heart more than with words. Indeed, she left an indelible mark in their lives. No doubt, the Potawatomi children appreciated her compassion, and those who watched her praying silently were deeply moved by her comomunion with God.

Today God's voice is calling us deep in our hearts to rise up against all odds. The assurance that all depends on God, not our own effort, gives us courage and opens our eyes to see everywhere opportunities that are opening up as an invitation to move towards a new world, to walk the unfamiliar plains, rocky grounds, mountains and jungles to meet so many hearts that are waiting to be touched and loved. ༺

Image: Waldemar Flaig

Following the Star

Maria Y., RSCJ
Province of Korea-Chinese

"Go into all the world and proclaim the good news to the whole of creation." (Mk 16:15)

Mission starts here. Philippine Duchesne was the pioneer RSCJ missionary to reach a new frontier. Returning to my own homeland as an RSCJ, I am aware that I walk in her footsteps.

In my journey of life, there has always been a star placed by God in front of me. The star gives me direction. It is not always very bright, but it is enough for me to see. God's voice is soft, but very strong. The moment a person hears the voice of God and follows the star may be a "Rebecca" moment, like the one Philippine Duchesne experienced when she boarded the ship named *Rebecca* after hearing God's call. Such moments are full of difficulties, yet grace-filled.

Years ago, God's star appeared to me. I followed it and left my hometown for an unknown land. With confusion, uncertainty, and fear I went, because God called. The day when I realised that God was with me in the Society of the Sacred Heart, all fears and doubts disappeared. Foreign cultures and languages enriched me. Through years of formation, I was moulded into a new creature.

Inspired by the zeal of Philippine Duchesne and the deliberation of the Society's international meeting in 2016, we sense a new "Rebecca" moment "to discover and reveal the love of the Heart of Jesus" on new frontiers. The star appears again.

Now I have been sent to my home country to begin the Duchesne Project. Because of my long absence, things in my homeland are totally new for me. It will take some time to adjust to new cultures and ways of life. It will take time to communicate with people. But God's star leads me to the place where my heart is to dwell. ❧

Image: Maria Korytko, RSCJ
Province of Poland

The Wise Men's Star

Boguslawa Ochal, RSCJ
Province of Poland

I have chosen a single small event from the history of the beginning of the missionary life of Saint Philippine Duchesne, without which, probably, the further history would not exist. One day, when Philippine was in the girls' dormitory (January 10, 1806), she was contemplating the detachment of the wise men. This was the moment when she desired to follow in their footsteps. A sign that she considered a confirmation of the true desire was the feeling of internal freedom. She desired to devote herself to preaching to non-believers.

To do so, like the wise men, she had to set out on a journey and start to look for Jesus in an unknown land. This "setting out," however, did not take place instantly. It was subject to Saint Madeleine Sophie's discernment with her and involved a wide range of feelings: expectations, prayer, desires, impatience.... Despite difficulties, Philippine remained faithful to the desire that was born during contemplation. In the end, she was given permission to set out like the wise men and travel a long distance. Contrary to that of the wise men, her journey was one-way travel. She stayed on another continent, consequently looking for Jesus and serving him until the end of her days, even when she did not see the light of the star.

Often, I wonder how deep and true this experience of meeting Jesus must have been that it gave her the strength that supported her through her entire life.

There are moments in the life of every one of us when desires are born during prayer. It is worth asking oneself when observing Saint Philippine: how long have I been already looking for Jesus? Do I still follow the star?

Image: Masako Egawa, RSCJ
Piles of black bags filled with radiation-contaminated soil stretching far and wide.

Thinking of Philippine in Fukushima

Masako Egawa, RSCJ
Province of Japan

Philippine Duchesne was moved by a strong call from God to go and be with native people in North America. Passion to bring the love of God led her to a land and people unknown to her. She travelled by ship, which took her two months – no internet, no smart phone, no Skype. While in America, she had to wait and wait for the letters from Sophie Barat. Faith, courage, and patience enabled her to carry on her mission to spread the love of the Heart of God.

Today it is easier for us to go anywhere, to reach out to people living at a distance. However, not far from us, people live far away from these benefits. The tsunami survivors with whom I have been sharing stories for a number of years are such people.

Here in Fukushima, Japan, after the triple disaster of earthquake, tsunami, and the nuclear power plant accident, in March 2011, countless people, after all these years, are still forced to live in a very tough situation. They do not know what their life will be like, when they will be able to go back to their own town, or when they can find jobs in a safer place. They have few certainties at all.

Newcomers cannot understand fully the suffering of these survivors. However, at least, we can be with them – to walk, to cry, or to laugh with them, even when we do not have the language to show our feelings towards them. Isn't this how we too, like Philippine, can spread the love of the heart of God and show that God is always with us?

Image: Dr. Hubert Zierl, Berchtesgaden

Roots and Branches

Ilsemarie Weiffen, RSCJ
Germany, Province of Central Europe

Strong as an oak tree and at the same time flexible in the face of any changes and challenges – this is Philippine Duchesne. It is not only her name that evokes an oak tree; it is even more her character – or is it more than that? Is it her rootedness in God?

The oak tree sends its roots deep into the earth, which makes it strong, resistant to heavy winds and severe thunderstorms. At the same time, the oak tree can adjust to different conditions, such as changes of climate.

Especially in her early years, Rose Philippine Duchesne had to overcome many difficulties, which challenged her not to give up but to adapt to different situations: called to religious life soon after her First Communion, she had to overcome her father's objections to her entering the convent. Having entered the Visitation convent of Sainte Marie-d'en-Haut at last, she was forced by the French Revolution, along with all the nuns, to leave the convent. Philippine returned to her family and looked after the poor and sick of the city, until she got into contact with Madeleine Sophie Barat, the founder of the Religious of the Sacred Heart.

What gave her the energy not to give up but to follow her initial vocation? Was it her strong will or rather was it her rootedness in God that gave her the strength to persevere despite all difficulties and failures? This rootedness let her reach out into the whole world, as the oak tree stretches out its branches. ❧

Image: Patricia Reid, RSCJ
Province of the United States-Canada

Facing the Unknown

Dorothea Hewlett, RSCJ
Province of Australia-New Zealand

Rebecca feels the breeze
stirring the ribbons on your travel-hat
and soon you will be summoned
ALL ABOARD!
Sophie consents at last, and blesses you.
How painful these last moments!
vineyard – and tumbril – weigh
upon your lonely sacrifice, as France recedes
and Indians call in language quite unknown;
but very soon they'll know you through and through,
Woman who always prays! Pray then for us; we too
bring the essential from our heritage
leaving the rest, as we set sail
for new life, a new land.

Image: Юлия Корнева
GettyImages.com

What Boat Must We Take?

Esperanza Calabuig, RSCJ
Cuba, Province of the Antilles

All of us in the Sacred Heart family are invited by the General Chapter to cross new frontiers. This means being alert like sentinels scanning the horizon, so that we are ready to love that territory most distant from us and feel "pulled" so that we swing into action. To go to these frontiers also means being ready to let go of the places where we are sent, being open to what is new, welcoming what we are discovering, examining it and praying about it before God. We need first to make plans so as to reach those new "territories," to become poor in spirit, acknowledging our ignorance, we need to take off our shoes and ask permission to approach that which is unknown to us.

I put "territories" in quotation marks because they can be either physical places or personal inner places. Often we don't know what transport to take, what visa to get, what entry permission; sometimes we need someone to help us. For example, how do we manage to cross borders blocking access to persons or peoples when consumerism is the most important thing? How do we reach the territories of people who are moved only by visible, tangible things and do not trust that what is best within them and is struggling to emerge will in fact make them happier? How do we help them discover – beyond distrust, low self-esteem, depression – this Spirit, with capital letter S, who is within each person and who desires to lead us to say ABBA?

And if difficulties arise when we glimpse something new, let us learn from Philippine to continue listening to the call, nourishing it, and praying as she did, not losing the opportunity to work on what will enable us to sail forth on our particular *Rebecca*.

Image: Mossolainen Nikolai
Shutterstock.com

None of This Is Reassuring If We Do Not See God in the Storm

Sandra Cavieres, RSCJ
Province of Chile

"The creaking masts, the sails hastily folded or torn to pieces, the helm abandoned in order to ease the ship, none of this is reassuring if we do not see God in the storm."
(Baunard, *Life of Mother Duchesne*, 212)

Philippine, an energetic woman, a lover of truth, did not hesitate to describe what was not "beautiful" in the *Rebecca's* journey. She says in a letter, "I shall not conceal from you the dangers of the sea nor my own weakness."

What an invitation to us to communicate truthfully the reality of our daily "journeys"! The storms that invade our lives today: violence, death, fanaticism, exclusion, apathy, difficulties that bring out our weaknesses, fragilities, fears. How can I discover God in my storm? How can I see with God's eyes? For Philippine, God was in all those signs of nature. She drew strength, she had four companions she had to support, especially Sister Catherine Lamarre, who was suffering and felt she could not continue the journey. Philippine sang the *Ave Maris Stella*. People said she had a lovely voice and the captain of the *Rebecca* insisted that she sing this beautiful song because it attracted good weather.

What are our "songs" to attract good weather? The song became prayer, in abandonment, in the certainty that God was there ... as on the Sea of Galilee.

My favorite prayer is community prayer ... there the storm is stilled. ❧

Image: Kathleen Hughes, RSCJ
Province of the United States-Canada

Handling a Broken Heart

Bonnie Kearney, RSCJ
Province of the United States-Canada

"Strong was her heart that heard God's voice when first it called across the seas." This is the first line of the song often sung on Philippine's feast, but it does not really reflect how that heart became so strong, many years before the call "across the seas." Philippine's heart exercised its love and service in her family, her neighborhood, her community at Sainte-Marie before the call to the New World came. Her life with the community on her beloved mountain taught her love and then, with events of the Revolution unfolding on every side, broke her heart, demanding that she leave, that she come down from the mountain.

There are many ways to handle a broken heart; Philippine's way was to put it into loving service. She may have left her mountain and her community, but she did not leave her commitment to serve as Jesus did. She sought the poor with clothing, the hungry with food, those in fear with a place to find shelter and hope. She cared for the poor, the children, the sick; and as she did, her broken heart became stronger, more compassionate, turned outwards, away from what she so longed for, to what her beloved longed to share with her. God's voice called and formed her into a servant of all, long before she felt the urging to come to the New World.

The New World would test her love and find only that her heart, even when broken again, set about becoming whole by loving more deeply, more widely, in silence, in prayer, in little actions of everyday life. Her life asks us to reflect on what we do when we feel our hearts breaking. Are we so sure that our God is Love itself broken, emptied, that we, too, set out to mend our tiny mirrors of that Heart, through service, compassion, interest in the other, recognition of the common humanity of all people? ❧

Image: Silvana Dallanegra, RSCJ

Philippine's Cross

Silvana Dallanegra, RSCJ
Province of England-Wales

When RSCJ make their perpetual profession of vows, they receive a cross to wear. This is a photo of the cross given to Philippine; it has been stored in our central archives in Rome since 1914.

It may well have spent the past century resting in a box, but with its worn insignia and mottos, it bears the imprint of the many years it has spent on mission. This is a cross that spent two months being battered by Atlantic winds and sprayed with salty water as it crossed the ocean in 1818. Year after year, it endured primitive conditions, mud, humidity and extremes of weather – bitter winter frosts and melting summer heat. Time and again it was clasped in times of crisis, disappointment or difficulty, maybe by hands damp with sweat or tears, providing a welcome reassurance of God's faithful love and presence. It reached new lands and crossed frontiers, spent hours in infirmaries and classrooms, lived in basic log cabins, cramped quarters and with Native Americans, and knew hours and whole nights spent in still, heartfelt prayer.

By 1852, as Philippine lay dying, this cross must have felt its years of service were coming to an end. And then Anna du Rousier arrived from France, en route to Chile, to begin the first Latin American foundation. She and Philippine exchanged profession crosses, and so Philippine's cross went with Anna on the long, arduous journey to a new frontier, trekking for months on tracks and bumpy roads, being bounced and thrown about each time her horse stumbled or she fell.

So much prayer, suffering, passion, fidelity, courage, and endeavor are ingrained in this cross, as surely as the insignia and mottos engraved on it. And just as it must have reminded Philippine of her vowed commitment, so it quietly reminds us today of the totality of her gift of herself and the call we all share with her, to give our whole lives to knowing and making known the unlimited love of the Heart of Jesus. ❧

Image: Anonymous, from St. Michael's Louisiana

Virtues Needed to Cross Frontiers:
Prayer, Missionary Zeal and Humility

Penina Ann Wambale, RSCJ
Province of Uganda-Kenya

Prayer shaped Philippine's life, helping her to embrace only what was essential in life, God's promptings. Prayer propelled Philippine to leave her comfortable family to become a religious, totally given to those on the margins of society. It gave her a certain resilience and audacity to leave her own country and go to America and, together with her companions, to become the first missionary of the Society of the Sacred Heart. Prayer increased her love and trust in Jesus; she would say, "She who has Jesus has everything."

Even at the age of seventy-one, when she was not able to do much, she accompanied her sisters and other people with prayer. Philippine was filled with missionary zeal; but her inability to speak the language of the people she loved and other difficulties she encountered show us a woman who accepted, even embraced, her limitations with the humility that enabled her to draw out the goodness from those she touched.

The image strikingly communicates Philippine's God-centered life, how she drew strength, zeal, humility, wisdom, and all the graces needed from the Heart of God. Philippine's passion to cross frontiers impels us to move out of our familiar comfort zones and open the doors of our hearts to those suffering in myriad ways around us and beyond our physical boundaries. We need to pay attention, to act as a body attending to the needs of those who knock at our doors, inviting us to cross our socio-cultural, political, and economic frontiers. She shows us how. May we dare to follow in Philippine's footsteps. ❧

Image: Pixabay.com

Philippine at a Crossroad

Teresa Gomà, RSCJ
Province of Spain

To write about Philippine is to focus our gaze on someone who stood out because of her persistence. A valiant and determined woman, she overcame many hardships with the strength of one who knows she possesses a truth, that of the love of God, which must be known further afield by more people. We discover this persistence in her early vocation at the age of twelve, in her admiration for Saint Francis Xavier, in Grenoble as a Visitation novice, in her deep friendship with Madeleine Sophie, in the obedience that kept her in France until she was forty-nine. Her strength is in her character, in her way of being, but also in the message that set her heart on fire.

Philippine was a woman who was all passion, but on her own she would probably have never achieved her aims. What was lacking was something unexpected, a chance event, or the Providence of God. On January 14, 1817, she was in charge of the portry of the motherhouse in Paris. She received a visitor for Madeleine Sophie, Bishop William Valentine Dubourg. She met the new bishop of Louisiana and Florida and knew that the great moment she had been expecting had arrived. When the bishop asked for religious for his new diocese, Madeleine Sophie accepted his request. It was May 16, 1817, and the moment had come to let Philippine go. She experienced tremendous joy.

The necessary human will and the overshadowing grace of God are two paths that come together at an unexpected point. Today, as then, the God of fidelity bursts into our lives. Let us always live in readiness, attentive to discover him at the crossroads. ✒

Image: Pixabay.com

Toward the Unknown

Rachele Gulisano, RSCJ
Province of Italy

One who starts out toward the unknown does not see the difficulties of the path right away because the gaze is directed in the distance. So Philippine, when she embarked on the *Rebecca* on March 21, 1818, and sailed toward an unknown world, was nearly fifty years old; but she had the energy of youth, the urgency to carry the Gospel to those who did not know it, and a heart full of hope. She did not yet know that often the plans of God do not coincide with ours, even though the French Revolution beforehand and the long wait afterwards had prepared her. Later, other painful events would remind her that "if the seed does not die, it will not bear fruit." And then, alongside simple people who spoke a language incomprehensible to her, she would be known for her silence, her full immersion in prayer.

But along the way, she would encounter other dangerous setbacks: practical difficulties, the climate, the food, the slowness of the mail, health ever more fragile, relationships that were not easy, and finally ... Mother Galitzine. who as visitator general in 1840 representing Madeleine Sophie, made decisions that were unwise and painful for Philippine. In this way, the intrepid Mother Duchesne, by the way of suffering, humiliation and prayer, arrived at that fullness of the gift of self that transformed her.

I think that Philippine is a great woman, not only for her apostolic zeal, but for the way in which she let herself be led, bent, and nearly shattered by great and small circumstances. Across the length of her long and difficult life, she always obeyed, God above all, but also superiors and religious and civil law, because she understood that the mission entrusted to her was that of "bearing witness to the love of the Heart of Jesus" by word and action, but perhaps even more by humble, silent prayer. ❧

Image: William Schickel

Grace and Grit: Mysticism and the Cross

Nance O'Neil, RSCJ
Area of Indonesia

Can a painting shout and whisper? This one does.
It shouts of grace and grit; it whispers about the cross.

The starkness of the black and white habit, the angular, almost ugly face express the austerity that characterized Philippine. Yet there is a softness that speaks, too. I think the quality communicated is grit. Her beatification process spoke of Philippine's "severe mortification" with all that connotes of Jansenism and masochism. The woman in this painting has all the grit and determination needed to follow through on her vision yet does not seem centered on self as the Jansenist and masochist must be. All through her life she had the grit to do what needed doing no matter what the cost. It was what needed doing that called forth that self-denying strength we identify with her. The painting has a mystical quality. The almost bizarre stance of the head – simultaneously facing in and out of the bonnet – says "the 'within' and 'without' are one." It is hard to tell which way she faces. The impression is of a woman worldly-wise and other-worldly. It is not hard to imagine her as a woman of deep contemplative prayer.

The painting has a subtle message about the cross. Actually, there is no cross on this habit. Where it would be, over the heart, hangs an oak leaf. Muted in color and size, this "cross" does not focus our attention. Whether the artist intended it or not, I don't know, but this treatment speaks to me. The cross is an oak leaf. In French, of course, Duchesne means "of oak." The message is that her very self was her cross – as is the case, I suspect, with most of us. There is a subtle peace about this oak leaf over her heart. There is nothing startling about there being a leaf where a cross should be. The painting whispers a message to me. Accepting a nature – with all the flaws and flamboyance we know to be Philippine's – has transformed the very core of her being into both the heart and cross of Christ. ❧

Image: Harry Webber

Truest Joy

Mary Hotz, RSCJ
Province of the United States-Canada

To those of us who think we are too old to do something, we have only to look to Philippine Duchesne for inspiration. At nearly fifty, she left home for Louisiana, and at seventy-two she trekked to Sugar Creek, Kansas, to live among the Potawatomi. When, at a certain moment, we may say, like the disciples on Mount Tabor, "We will sit down now and do no more," Philippine invites us to move off the mountain into the mud of life, from altitude to sea level, from Grenoble and Paris to New Orleans and St. Louis. When, amid despair and powerlessness, when language fails us, Philippine, the woman of unceasing prayer, beckons us to courage and confidence born from unceasing contemplation, as if to say, "Excuse me, but we have God's work to do." ❧

Image: Maria Stecka, RSCJ

The New Frontier

Maria Stecka, RSCJ
Province of Poland

"Domine, in simplicitate cordis meus laetus obtuli universa …"

After the fall of communism in Russia, Moscow became a special place of mission for RSCJ. In the time of Philippine, numbers of residents of the village of Florissant were baptized each Easter. Every year, numbers of adults, prepared by the RSCJ of Moscow, receive the sacraments of Christian initiation at Easter.

After the Revolution, France needed "workers" for a new evangelization, but the call of America was still more important to Philippine because the Indian peoples had heard nothing of the Good News of God. "Here I am!" was Philippine's answer.

Philippine encountered many difficulties in the New World: poverty, sickness, hard work, loneliness, and resistance to religion because of what Philippine considered loose morals. In all those contradictions a LIVELY FAITH was her support. This faith was expressed for her by obedience through an ongoing relationship with Sophie. It was also expressed in an honest dialogue with the clergy of Louisiana.

The fruitfulness of her labours came from her acceptance of suffering of all kinds, of humiliations and failures. Her consolation came from long hours of prayer at night before the Blessed Sacrament, where she drew new strength and peace from the Heart of Jesus. *"It is less by succeeding than by putting up with setbacks, that you are destined to please me,"* she heard one day during prayer.

The rebirth of the Church in Russia challenges languages, cultures, and many nations on the borders between Europe and Asia. We must respond as RSCJ. Urged by the call to cross frontiers, let us be guided forward! ❧

Image: Shutterstock.com

Learning from Philippine, Woman of Faith

Henni Sidabungke, RSCJ
Area of Indonesia

What comes to mind when you hear Philippine's name? This question surfaced one day for us when younger members of the Indonesian region had gathered. We were delighted to learn that the Indonesian mission began when Philippine was canonized. We are blessed that Philippine, a woman of courage and faithfulness, is patron of our area.

To imagine what Philippine and her companions felt during their voyage to the New World helps us to understand that they were all woman of faith. They saw only the sea and sky. They suffered from illness; they had no appropriate food. The sea terrorized them with winds and waves. Uncertainty awaited in the new land. Philippine's close relationship with Jesus sustained her and enabled her to live with hope during these perilous times. Her prayer, "My God, I have left all things for you," reveals that she was a woman whose heart was united with God long before the Potawatomi said so.

We experience terrifying moments like hers nowadays, but in different ways. When we leave home to seek what God wants of us, we are uncertain and fearful. When everything seems uncertain, when people feel hopeless, when hatred and jealousy increase while love and forgiveness decrease, can we become a sign of hope for people around us?

Philippine shows the way. Strength for the journey of life comes from contemplation of the pierced Heart of Jesus. May the Love of the Heart of Jesus, which sustained Philippine, mold us to be holy and to be a blessing for others! ❧

Image: Margaret Mary Nealis, RSCJ
Province of Canada

Living with Philippine's Heart

N'guemta Nakoye Mannta (Juliette), RSCJ
Province of Chad

I came to know Philippine Duchesne through stories told by one or other RSCJ, and from writings about her. Later I had the grace of visiting some places where she lived in the United States. With Philippine Duchesne, I have seen how my life is a physical, intellectual, human, psychic and spiritual journey with an open heart, like Abraham, moving towards myself, others, nature and God with a deep inner joy. Something I continue to experience linked with her in contemplating her picture on the *Rebecca*, is her openness in crossing cultural, religious, North/South and social frontiers.

Setting out with nothing at the start of her mission, Philippine teaches me that real human poverty is not a lack of money, but rather the lack of heart or of love towards others. As Helder Camara puts it, "Nobody is so poor that he has nothing to offer; nobody is so rich that [she] does not need help." By her person, Philippine enriches each of us. Temple of the living God, Philippine Duchesne has enabled me to see, through her being, that "to discover and manifest the love of the Heart of Christ by the service of education" is a universal heritage lived daily by every RSCJ and by everyone who decides to live by it. ❧

Image: Adam Long

Beyond the Limits of Our Sight

Kim King, RSCJ
Province of the United States-Canada

Philippine dreamed big and listened wide for the voice, the call, of God. Whether working with those in need closer to home in Grenoble, or giving herself to a pull that would take her away from that which was physically familiar and ever deeper into the diverse terrain of the Heart where she made her true home, Philippine responded with *disponibilité*, creativity, and a broad, inclusive desire to make God's love known.

With fervor, she talked and wrote openly of her desires, her thoughts, her discernment with God. My contemporary imagination easily hears her saying year after year "and, oh, by the way… if you need someone to cross an ocean and start something new… I'm still open because that is where I believe God is calling me to go."

It is one thing to have the dream. It is another still to voice it. But it is something else altogether to drop everything and go forward once approval comes… to go when the cost is dear and the unknowns looming; to go prayerfully and with courage; to say Yes and walk on knowing that doubt, fear, and challenge will be probable companions and might sometimes even gain the upper hand temporarily; to say Yes, above all else, to sharing the Love to which I too have given my life.

That level of freedom, that intensity of commitment to dreaming and discerning, to the Society, to God, and to God's people, is one of the qualities I admire most about Philippine.

Image: Milton Frenzel

Staying

Paula Grillo, RSCJ
Province of Argentina-Uruguay

I think that Philippine would be very surprised by the admiration and inspiration that she arouses in us. Years ago, when I heard about her for the first time, I was impressed by her desire to be a missionary. I was struck by the fact that, with all that needed to be done in her country, with the great needs and challenges of the society of her time, she looked beyond her own frontiers and wanted to bring the love of the Heart of Christ "to the ends of the earth".

It has always seemed to me a great risk, full of courage, to decide to leave everything and to cross the immense ocean, knowing that it would be almost impossible to return. I admired her courage and the deep desire that encouraged her to embark on this voyage.

Now, years after first knowing her story, I discover that what I love most about her is what happened afterwards: meeting the practical difficulties of this new country where she had arrived, suffering from the lack of understanding of her own sisters, having to wait so long to live with the indigenous people for whom she longed to be in mission, and not to be able to learn their language. And on this journey, so full of obstacles, Philippine remained rooted in the love of Jesus, that love that had driven her on this adventure and that accompanied her in the midst of apparent failure.

When I think of how to be faithful to our charism today, I admire Philippine's daring, but I also pray for her ability to stay in the midst of difficulties, to stay close to those realities that make us touch our own limits, to know how to embrace misunderstandings and mistakes, because there too a sacred space is revealed to us where we can discover and reveal the love of the One who loves us and wants to give us life in abundance so that we may share it with all God's sons and daughters. ❧

Image: Microsoft clipart

Woman with a Global Heart

Maureen Glavin, RSCJ
Province of the United States-Canada

I find Philippine Duchesne to be a particularly inviting model for our twenty-first century world because she had a global heart.

A global heart shifts the focus of interest and compassion from "me" to "us" to "all of us"! This development describes an emergence of consciousness and compassion into ever-expanding circles. The circle of "my neighbor" is an ever-increasing number of people with whom I am capable of truly empathizing. A global heart has an inclusive, wide tent and a porous boundary!

Philippine Duchesne was constantly expanding the boundaries of her heart. As a child she yearned to reach out to the poor of Grenoble; as an adolescent and a young nun she dreamed of working with native peoples across the ocean; as an old woman she longed to travel to the Rocky Mountains and beyond – even to China. Philippine courageously crossed frontiers that were not just geographic or political; she crossed frontiers of social class, language, culture, and custom. Philippine's circle of compassion was as wide as the world. Her deep desire was to bring the Love of God, which she had come to know so intimately, to those in the world she thought were most removed from it. Philippine had a Global Heart.

So what of us? How broad is the tent of our own inclusion? How wide is the circle of our compassion? How porous are the boundaries of our hearts? For whom do our hearts hurt? If the answer is too narrow or parochial, it is useful to remember how Philippine's heart became so global. How? She opened her heart. She spent copious amounts of time allowing God's Love, through Christ, to fill her, to form her and, ultimately, to transform her. Philippine's heart thus became increasingly revelatory of Christ's Heart. And like Christ's Heart, her heart encompassed the globe. ❧

Image: Emil Frei

Silence

Ursula N. Bugembe, RSCJ
Province of Chad

Philippine's life is marked by many qualities. What stands out for me is her silence, which attracted many in her day and still seizes our hearts today. This legacy of silence was at the heart of Philippine's life, enabling her to remain focused on the Lord's ways interiorly and to act radically. The interior life she lived enabled her to risk new frontiers in response to calls of her time. She lived a life like that of Mary the mother of Jesus. Philippine's silence is a lesson we want to understand as we navigate our own lives. We want to be silent interiorly and present to others, even though not using many words. Her extraordinary way of living daily in deep contemplation enabled her to grow in union with Jesus.

I pray that Philippine intercede for us so that we too may grow in interior life for mission, wherever God sends us. Even if the ordinary language of communication fails, dear Philippine, let your example and God's graces make us believe in the quality of silence. May we walk fearlessly into untrodden paths to discover a language without words that seizes our hearts for things of God. Pray for us to remain anchored in our source of life, the Lord, who prepared you for mission in the New World. The Lord had all the instruments needed implanted in the storehouse of your heart. May you obtain for us the same graces to help us wait patiently, silently, and trustingly as God is preparing our hearts for new frontiers, our new callings today in the twenty-first century. ❧

Image: Andrei Rublev

A Community of Three

Stella S., RSCJ
Province of Korea-Chinese

My first community was named "Duchesne," and it was on the Feast of Philippine that I entered the novitiate in the Philippines. Since then Philippine has had a place in my heart, and I have been deeply inspired by her life of prayer and zeal for mission. From her story, I learned that her first desire for mission was to go to my country, but that God had another plan for her. With all these connections, I felt close to her and often turned to her for help.

Four years ago, after my final profession, I was sent to my homeland for mission. I was excited but also filled with fear and uncertainty. I was afraid of being alone, without a community. Also, my presence was no longer just as an individual but as a member of the Society. This was a weight on my heart.

On the airplane, I read a small book written by Janet Erskine Stuart, RSCJ. Each word spoke to me deeply. I started to feel the strong connection with the Society and especially the presence of Sophie and Philippine. I conversed with them about many things, especially on the life of prayer and on failure, the latter often Philippine's experience. This gave me much strength and courage for the journey.

Before leaving the plane, I realized that I was in a community of three – Sophie and Philippine had joined me. Together we would start a new mission. This mission is now called the Duchesne Project. How blessed I am to be a member of this community! ❧

Image: Timothy Schnalz

To Be and To Act as One Body

Nancy Koke, RSCJ
Province of Uganda-Kenya

The Society has recently called us "to act as one body…" moved from its center by Love. Within this body, life flows, weaving different kinds of connections, bringing energy and flexibility to each part. What affects one of these parts affects the whole body.
—General Chapter of the Society of the Sacred Heart, 2016, p. 15.

It was a great sacrifice for Sophie to allow Philippine and her companions to go to the New World, but she realized how important it was to respond to the calls of the Church and the world. Sophie understood that Philippine and her companions would remain part of the one body of the Society. The *Cor Unum* was made stronger through their mission in another part of the world and the correspondence between France and the New World. Although Philippine often had to wait for months before hearing from France, her loyalty to Sophie and the Society led her to maintain the sense of one body at all costs, even when decisions contravened her own wishes. Her humility and desire to follow the Spirit allowed her to "let go," to yield to the opinion of others; but when the oneness of the Society was at stake, she was adamant.

Philippine must be very happy with the Chapter's call to unity, especially when she sees our efforts to answer it in the concrete circumstances of our lives. May she intercede for us to enable us to grow as one body in our relationships with one another and with our God, who calls us to be of one mind and one heart in the Heart of Jesus.

Image: Mary Verghese, RSCJ

Crossing Boundaries – Breaking Barriers

Mary Varghese, RSCJ
Province of India

Philippine Duchesne offers us the heart of a "frontier woman." She was a woman of deep prayer, as others described her, and a woman who spoke with her heart in the Saint Charles and Florissant world of her time. She was undaunted by language, culture, climate, distances, and uncertainties of every kind. Instead, like a humble seed in the earth, she garnered a rich harvest in the slow process of dying and birthing.

Over the centuries, like Philippine, many young women and men felt "a call to mission" in distant lands and made immeasurable contributions in these places. Today, however, in several countries, missionaries are not so welcome. Their work is often considered controversial and their presence experienced as a threat to certain age-old traditions and cultures. Moreover, the internet is a great means of communication today. So, where do the frontiers exist? What would the "frontier woman" be like today?

Perhaps Philippine, our frontier woman, has a question or two for us: Do we need to strengthen our internal bonds – spiritual and material? At the same time, should we turn outward to new life-giving sources, there to discover our place and spirituality anew? Where, for example, do we see ourselves in relation to the young who are being drawn by the Spirit to differently expressed spiritual commitments and involvement in the service of humanity?

Saint Philippine calls us today to respond to the promptings of the Spirit. In this lies our hope. How best can we address these realities in the midst of uncertainties and even, humanly speaking, at the risk of possible failure? Philippine beckons us to courage, unceasing prayer and contemplation in order to let go of all that hinders us and to let come the powerful work of the Spirit in our lives. ❧

Philippine: the woman who prays always

Allow us to draw near very quietly,
while you pray, caught up in this thirsting world
and to learn as you did, the wise way
of serving the water that springs up from the Eternal.
May we be always watchful
and allow God to pour forth his torrent
and reinvigorate the development of a people
who are seeking solutions in the puddles
and are unable to find in our lives
the overflowing selflessness of God.
Help us to pray as you did
to pay the price of silence
and to receive joyfully the gift of a prayer
in which God's gift of self
overflows among God's people.

— Estela Henao, RSCJ

Image: Milton Frenzel

The Woman Who Prays Always

Estela Henao, RSCJ
Province of Colombia

Since we were children, educated in a Sacred Heart school, we learned to recognize the name of Philippine Duchesne as the first missionary of the congregation, without many details, but we knew of whom we were speaking.

Now, as a religious, the invocation of this outstanding woman is embedded in my heart; she was courageous in feeling herself insignificant, the good sister of the community who hastened to offer her services without being noticed, who tenderly welcomed the little ones in the school, and who made up for the difficulty of making herself understood in a language that she never mastered.

One wonders how she was able to pass just as one among others, without the gift of a foreign language, but the Potawatomi give us the clue: she was the woman whose silence spoke volumes. That is her great gift, not just to our congregation but to the Church and the world of today. She gave that powerful witness of being the woman in whom people felt and experienced the presence of God.

The truly effective witness is that of a life in which the greatness of the humility of God vibrates. The deep and effective lesson of total self-giving in Jesus, who accepted to become one of us: limited but not worthless, powerless but not useless, close to us yet containing all the potential of the Trinitarian God, is what Philippine understood and what we and all the family of the Sacred Heart feel and love. ❧

Image: Maureen Hansen, Stuartholme, Brisbane

Lights on Philippine Duchesne

Moira Donnelly, RSCJ
Province of Ireland-Scotland

Appeal to the Young. Some years ago, two boys aged about twelve came to our house to ask for help with their school project on religious life. We told them a few facts about our Society and gave them some booklets and pictures. A short time later, we were invited to their exhibition. On entering the hall, our attention was drawn immediately to a six-foot high poster of Philippine sitting on the deck of the *Rebecca*; and in their presentation, the boys made clear by their enthusiasm that Philippine was just the kind of religious they could understand and admire. Her daring, dedication, and her selfless loving had captured their imagination. I learned from children that day a new appreciation for the gift to the Society of Philippine Duchesne.

Social Justice. In 1988, I had the privilege of making a pilgrimage organized by our French sisters. We visited the great house in Grenoble where the Duchesne and Perier families grew up, Philippine's beloved Sainte-Marie d'En-Haut, and the Grande Chartreuse high in the majestic Alps. But the place that left the strongest impression on me was the Chateau de Vizille. In 1988, many banners around Vizille proclaimed it "Le Berceau de la Révolution!" ("The Cradle of the Revolution"). On display was the Charter of Human Rights, drawn up there in 1788, a document that triggered the Revolution and was partly the work of Philippine's Uncle Claude. How much did Philippine hear of the political discussions going on around her? How did this affect her championship of the poor and the oppressed? For me, Vizille opened another window into the mind and heart of Philippine.

The Pioneer. The third memorable moment was my visit to Florissant on a bitterly cold March day. As I shivered in the spacious dormitory, my companion spoke to me about life in the boarding school in Philippine's time. She assured me that things would have been even more austere then. As she spoke, I imagined Philippine walking around at night, trying to bring comfort and warmth to the pupils, then going to break the ice on the water jugs. Sitting in that comfortless room, I felt over-awed by the sheer heroism of this valiant woman. ❧

*Image: "Round House" at the Academy of the Sacred Heart, St. Charles, Missouri.
Early burial place of Rose Philippine Duchesne.*

My Friendship with Philippine

Helen Rosenthal, RSCJ
Province of the United States-Canada

Rose Philippine Duchesne was beatified in 1940. Four years later, at age thirteen, I began high school as a weekly boarder at the Academy of the Sacred Heart in St. Charles, Missouri. The school was first opened by Philippine in 1818. Each night, I was one of the students who went to close up the shrine where Philippine was buried. Sometimes we would be wrapped up in the nuns' black shawls to go out and say goodnight to our "Mother Duchesne." I think I learned to pray as we knelt around the marble tomb with only flickering light from the amber and green vigil lights that decorated it. For me, Mother Duchesne was a real mother: tender, loving, interested in all that I did each day and ready to help me. Those nightly conversations began a real friendship with Philippine that continues even today.

When I was sent straight from Rome to Chile after my final profession, Philippine Duchesne accompanied me in a special way. It was her courage and fortitude that carried me through the first year when I struggled to control 157 middle school children without knowing the language. Philippine had managed to start schools without a command of the language, and so I turned to her for strength and to keep my sense of humor. Then, an earthquake destroyed our convent and school. While we were living without running water or electricity, the thought of what Philippine had suffered made it easy to stay cheerful. Philippine faced so many great hardships and stayed serene. Our friendship deepened as she helped me to find more time for prayer. My twenty years as a missionary in Chile owe much to the example of our Saint. ❧

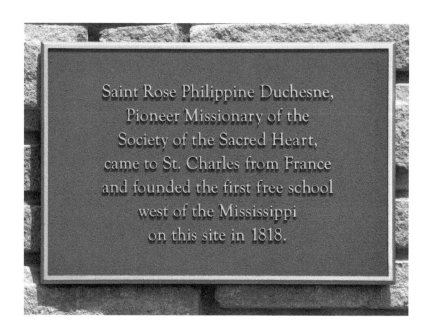

Academy of the Sacred Heart, St. Charles, Missouri
Image: Linda Behrens

"A Remarkable Woman ..."

Anne McCarthy, RSCJ
Province of England-Wales

Arriving in St. Charles, for a visit in 2001, I wandered into a gift shop in the town and was approached by an assistant. With pride she said, "There was a remarkable woman who lived here in the early days and now she is a saint." Then, noticing my medallion, she said, "Oh, you'll know all about her!"

Having led morning assembly on Philippine on at least twenty occasions and celebrated, in 1988, with staff and pupils her canonization, I did have plenty of knowledge about Philippine Duchesne. What I was to experience in the next three days was her spirit, as the RSCJ community shared the places and events of her life.

Philippine died in St. Charles in 1852, and yet, nearly 150 years later, there were signs of her all around: an information board about her on the river bank; the sign, shown opposite, indicating the site of Philippine's first school; signposts to the Sacred Heart Academy and her shrine.

While schools, communities, and a novitiate flourished elsewhere, Philippine's time at St. Charles was not a "success." The free school, housed in a rough log cabin, 1818-19, had to close; and when RSCJ were brought back by Jesuits after ten years, Philippine had to leave it to others to re-establish it.

When she moved to St. Charles, after her year with the Potawatomi, having been too old to learn their language, Philippine felt a failure and was in poor health. She spent her last ten years mending clothes, making vestments, and praying. The people knew and loved her as simple and humble, and today they still call her "a remarkable women!"

*Image: Saint Rose Philippine Producers' Cooperative logo
depicting the community sailing on with Philippine to new frontiers*

Philippine Duchesne in Ormoc

Iraida Sua-an, RSCJ
District of the Philippines

In 1991, about 8,000 lives were lost in flash floods in Ormoc, Philippines, because of the deforestation of the mountains and the wanton destruction of the environment. Religious of the Sacred Heart felt the need to respond to this terrible tragedy, and I was sent to help in the rehabilitation of the families that had lost their shelters and their loved ones, most of whom were exploited workers in a sugar cane plantation. From the beginning, Philippine Duchesne served as my silent guide and provider, for I felt that this mission frontier would be close to her heart.

Sacred Heart provinces around the world had spontaneously sent financial help, so we were able to acquire a one-hectare property and subdivide it among the families. For the first time in their lives, they could settle down in homes they could call their own. They continued to live simple and laborious lives, but they found hope for their daily needs in the words of Philippine: "God knows our need. He knows what we want and in His own time He will grant it."

A community gradually was organized with childhood education as its center. Here the children could receive the love and care of Philippine transmitted to them. Through their new life together, the whole community experienced a taste of the reign of God through peace and stability and a brighter future for their children.

After twenty-six years in Ormoc, the RSCJ are handing over the administration of the Saint Philippine Duchesne Ormoc Workers Foundation Incorporated (SPDOWFI), assured that the people have been empowered and that Philippine's mission will continue. As I leave, Philippine's words are etched in my heart: "We cultivate a very small field for Christ, but we love it, knowing that God does not require great achievements but a heart that holds back nothing for self.... The one who has Jesus has everything." ❧

Image: Artist Unknown

Philippine, Woman of Yesterday … Woman for Today

Isabel Rocha, RSCJ
Province of Argentina-Uruguay

When I think of Rose Philippine Duchesne as a person, with her courage and commitment, her need to go to the peripheries and her contemplative being, I am connected immediately to where we are today. She speaks as a woman of yesterday but with a deep, clear, solid perception that the world of today so needs.

Philippine could go step-by-step in fidelity to the Lord, a woman of profound hope in tumultuous and difficult times. She had hope, trust and fidelity for an unfolding future.

And it is that patient step-by-step approach that our world so needs. In times where immediacy, consumerism, and superficiality race together, we too are sometimes caught up in this race and unwittingly lose our very essence, our deepest identity, our freedom. There is no time for silence; there is no time for encounter. There is time for doing but not for being in the doing.

She knew how to be and manifest the love of the Heart of Jesus wherever she was. A woman of deep availability, she knew how to put herself aside so as to bring Jesus to the poor of the Kingdom.

Today, our times too are tumultuous and difficult, though in a different way. We live in a moment of history where there is more and more oppression, violence, inequality, and injustice, where there are more and more barriers. We live in a moment when Mother Earth cries out along with our brothers and sisters. This is a moment needing calculated risk-taking, generous availability, a loving look towards the margins. It is there that we find the Potawatomi of today. It is there that he awaits us – and they too await us.

Philippine, woman of yesterday, who speaks so much to us today, tells us that fidelity to God is the most important. It is that which brings us to the most fragile. It is that which enables us to overcome obstacles and incomprehension. It is that fidelity which empowers us to be loving as she loved and to live, out of love, in union and conformity with the Heart of Jesus.

When one lives like this, one can transcend everything, and we are capable of communicating in a different way, as she did. ❧

Image: Catherine Blood, RSCJ
Province of England-Wales

A Prayer to Philippine

Maria Cecilia Amarante, RSCJ
Province of Brazil

Full of courage in the face of suffering and misunderstandings,
obtain moral strength for us.
Humble, zealous, and unpossessive in friendship,
teach us to love with the Heart of Jesus Christ.
Tireless in the struggle for the Reign of Christ,
communicate your eagerness to us.
Living lesson on prayer, help us to live our spirituality
of incarnation and paschal mystery.
Inspirer of missionary love towards the poorest,
obtain for us zeal for the Kingdom.
Patient in awaiting the Lord's time, teach us hope.
Persevering in the engagement of causes for the indigenous,
open our heart to all our sisters and brothers.
Inimitable adorer of the Eucharistic Jesus, communicate to us
your desire for a total gift of ourselves.
Our herald to the Southern Hemisphere, obtain for us the grace
of a genuine option for the poor.
Example of poverty and total emptying of self,
teach us forgetfulness of self.
Saint Philippine, pray for us to the Heart of Jesus,
the one to whom you gave your life without reserve.

Image: Microsoft clipart

Philippine
Grain of Wheat Fallen into the Earth ...

Marie-Paule Préat, RSCJ
Province of Belgium-France-Netherlands

Philippine had only opened up the furrow and, with what difficulties, sown the seed... But one day the Sacred Heart would return and harvest it.... Her role was to open up the way through the brambles. She is God's pioneer (Msgr. Baunard).

Philippine's way was one of hiddenness. She landed in Louisiana, driven by the intuition of proclaiming Love to the ends of the earth; and at the age of forty-nine, she began a patient journey of sowing. She went forward in a discerning way, through requests and offers received, in a courageous dialogue with men of the Church who were given to her as co-workers and with feminine intuition. In spite of the abundant fruits and rapid growth of the mission, she seemed to see only its hidden and suffering face. She carried the cross with Jesus, while the Resurrection was already at work around her.

Our land today is rocky through its rejection of God and a culture of indifference but also fertilized by the thirst of humanity and the desire for ecological change. What furrow should we open up? What seed should we sow? Would the acceptance of fragility, modest and tentative participation in the searching of today's citizens, be crosses to be carried with Jesus, ways of burial necessary for a harvest that we shall not see with our own eyes? ❧

Image: Catherine Blood, RSCJ
Province of England-Wales

Philippine's Return to Sainte-Marie d'En-Haut

Colette Mercier, RSCJ
Province of Belgium-France-Netherlands

In 1801, in the midst of a glacial winter's cold, some Grenoble youngsters hanging around the streets were called by Philippine for a rather extraordinary task: to help her refurbish her dear Monastery of the Visitation, badly damaged by the French Revolution.

We see them carrying heavy packages.

We picture them cheerful and noisy …

The mission with these children was clearly received at the time of her pilgrimage to La Louvesc in May 1800, a village evangelized by Saint Francis Regis. She returned then, having decided to provide instruction for the poor, following the example of Saint Francis Regis.

Tenacity, courage, and generosity energized Philippine in this step, and even more, because "in the faces of these boys, I saw the reflection of the Lord's gaze," she stated.

A contemplative gaze? Yes, her whole happiness lay in being there, as it was on that blessed Holy Thursday night, April 1806: "I was happier among them than among all the grandees of the world."

Today? A mission always of today, according to Pope Francis: "Illiteracy still remains very present … a great injustice striking at the dignity of the human person. Instruction is truly a particular (special) form of evangelization."

With Philippine's tenacity, courage, and generosity, together with the strength of our charism, may we respond to this ever relevant call: to work for the integral development of the person, to build a world of justice and peace; and in response to the cry of the poor, to proclaim the Gospel. ❧

Image: Maribel Carceller, RSCJ

The "Rebecca Moment" in the Philippines

Maribel V. Carceller, RSCJ
District of the Philippines

Ever since Philippine Duchesne and her companions set sail for the New World on a ship named *Rebecca*, we have come to speak about "Rebecca moments" as times of choice, sometimes in perilous situations or when facing uncertainty about the future similar to what Philippine faced when she boarded the *Rebecca* in 1818.

In the Philippines our "Rebecca" moment came on August 22, 1969, when the first two Filipino RSCJ "set sail" from Japan in response to the Second Vatican Council's call for the renewal of religious life. It had been 151 years earlier on August 21, 1818, that Philippine Duchesne set foot on Market Street Landing in St. Louis, Missouri.

More Filipino RSCJ joined them to start a "little society," living in a rented apartment in the midst of the inner city of Manila and seeking to discover how religious life for them as RSCJ would take form. The community participated in political action and education for the next twenty years of martial law until the People Power Revolution overthrew the dictatorship in 1986.

Soon after, as our contribution to nation-rebuilding, we went to Northern Samar, one of the poorest and most neglected provinces of the Philippines. This year we celebrate thirty years of presence in this Duchesne-like mission.

Together, our little community of the Philippine District prayed, discerned decisions, and eventually evolved a post-Vatican religious life form that was considered a breakthrough in the lifestyle and ministries of the Society of the Sacred Heart. ❧

Window in St. Joseph Mission Church
Soboba Indian Reservation

The **Eagle** is Sacred—the carrier of our prayers to God.
The **Smoke** from the sage represents our prayers arising.
The **Acorns** symbolize the meal we celebrate, and
The **Gourd-rattle** is the music of our songs to God.

Prayer to Saint Philippine from Soboba Indian Reservation

Marianna Torrano, RSCJ
Province of the United States-Canada

O holy woman, who prays always, we honor you
You are like Eagle, soaring high to Creator
Your prayer is like sweet-smelling smoke of sage and cedar
Your presence with us is acorn meal, feeding our spirits and drawing us to Grandfather
O holy woman, who prays always, we thank you
You brought your Society to us long years ago
Your sisters are with us even now, in your name
Your love and prayer help us walk the Red Road
O holy woman, who prays always, we ask your blessing
Bless us, your Indian children, and stay with us always
Bless our land, Mother Earth, given by Creator
Bless all people who walk on Mother Earth. May we live together in peace.
Amen, Aho! ❧

Image: Hildreth Meière

We Can Make a Difference

Kaja Kayembe Clémentine, RSCJ
Province of Democratic Republic of Congo

In this image, Saint Rose Philippine stands between two girls in a position that is very significant. This image reminds me of many illiterate women, particularly in my part of the world, who are struggling to love and educate their children against many odds. I have always admired Philippine's courage. Even though she could not speak English, she founded schools in a predominately English-speaking country. She was a woman impelled to action for social justice. She never gave up the mission to Native Americans, for which she waited so long. Through these actions, she realized the encounter of two civilizations by fighting against illiteracy and poverty for God's sake. Philippine is my source of inspiration and courage, particularly in uncharted situations. She is a model teacher. I often ask what might have motivated Philippine Duchesne to love children and the poor.

I see a similarity between Philippine and Pope Francis, whose hearts are wide open to the most vulnerable. On his way back from Greece in 2017, Pope Francis brought home with him twelve Syrian refugees, all of them Muslims. These twelve are now receiving language and job training as well as educational opportunities. Recently, he organized a party for 1,500 economically disadvantaged people.

In most cases, a poor person is an outsider, a person to fear! When I consider what motivated Philippine in all her actions, my heart is grateful for God's unfailing love and for the gift of Philippine to the Society. I am convinced that only love can destroy barriers and create bridges between the poor and the rich. In Africa, some traditions have led people to perceive the materially poor and women as destitute and vulnerable. However, if educated, these groups of people become very capable and strong. I believe that the worst aspect of poverty is being illiterate. I pray that, as the Society of the Sacred Heart, we continue Philippine Duchesne's legacy, becoming more aware of the injustices caused by poverty in our own time. Through education, may we do all in our power to eliminate these injustices. ❧

Image: Donna Collins, RSCJ

With Dirt Under Her Fingernails

Donna Collins, RSCJ
Province of the United States-Canada

Philippine's attempts to reopen Sainte-Marie d'En-Haut must have demanded skills that were not normally in the repertoire of wealthy young women. Had she been observant of trades people or did she simply problem-solve when taking on practical tasks? When Sophie asked her to prepare the house on the Rue des Postes, we hear that she not only scrubbed and cleaned but replaced window panes and assisted in applying the mortar when the builders were too slow.

We know that after a few years on the American frontier, Philippine was mending furniture and had mastered gardening, milking, and mucking out the barn. When "difficult" children were sent out into the garden to spend time with her, whom did they meet? Philippine was that old nun with the mended habit and dirt under her nails. She was not piously snipping off a few daisy heads but laboring to produce vegetables for the table.

In the early foundations, such practical tasks were necessary for survival and none of them was beneath Philippine. She rose to each new occasion and accepted the challenges with generosity, good humor, intelligence, and a dash of Duchesne determination. There must have been errors and failures, but Philippine was not afraid to try. There would also have been occasions when her patience was tested in helping the impractical, the less competent, and those not as willing to get their hands dirty.

Are we willing to get dirt beneath our nails as we labor alongside Philippine? ❧

Image: Mag. Radoslaw Celewicz, Vienna

Darkness into Light

Ilsemarie Weiffen, RSCJ
Germany, Province of Central Europe

Dark and light, not knowing where to go, what to do, chaos or creation – what was it that Rose Philippine Duchesne had to face in her life?

She felt herself called to be a missionary, and it took her a long way until Madeleine Sophie Barat let her undertake the adventure of setting sail to North America. Longing to live with the Indians, she had, first of all, to deal with the children in Missouri. When, after an almost life-long journey, she went to the Potawatomi, she had to accept that she was not able to learn their language. But she didn't give up; she simply did what she could do, she prayed for them.

Philippine Duchesne didn't give up when she had to face difficulties or when she had to accept that her dreams were far from reality. She had the capacity to discover light in every darkness; she was able to find ways where there seemed to be no pathway. Going to the frontiers of her abilities, she didn't give up when she failed but opened herself to new horizons.

Is this the nature of a person who thinks positively? More than that, it is the strength of somebody who lets herself be guided by the Lord. It is the strength and the power of a woman who follows God through every darkness, step by step, trusting that every tunnel leads into light. Not her own will and desire determined what to do, but the reality in which she discovered God's call.

Image: Glenn Bahm

Our Timeless Source of Inspiration

Betty Susan Nankya Nsanja, RSCJ
Province of Uganda-Kenya

The map held by Rose Philippine Duchesne could not suffice; she needed the guidance of the Spirit. The Spirit led our dear Philippine to the unknown and to becoming our pioneer missionary to the Americas. This was the beginning of the outward movement of the Society of the Sacred Heart, the spread of her mission to many other lands, including Africa.

Her courage in crossing ever-new frontiers remains overwhelming! Philippine looks straight into our eyes, inviting us to respond to God's callings in our world today, troubled yet rich in God's graces. By her example, she reminds us that a journey marked by faith is never straight. Some days may be green and others grey, cloudy, sooty, and unbearable.

Against all the odds we face today, for example, wars, terrorism, the immigration crisis, climate change and its threat to human life, Philippine challenges us to dare not give up but to persevere until our dreams come to fruition. She is a voice whispering to us, sharing her impeccable, admirable spirit, calling us to live more humanly, united as one body.

May we set out, fearlessly, with our sails raised high, guided by God's map, with Jesus Christ on our *Rebecca*. Ours is a journey of faith, mapped out as we navigate our own high seas to reach new frontiers, where human life is being threatened and needs to be defended. We look upon you, Philippine, to intercede for us, to have the same zeal for prayer and readiness to set out, and to set sail as a whole family of the Sacred Heart to new frontiers that beckon in our hearts. ❧

Image: Students at candlelight demonstration in Korea
Photographer unknown

Education: A Frontier

Lim, Tae Youn, RSCJ
Province of Korea-Chinese

The missionary spirit of Philippine Duchesne is an endless source of inspiration, which stimulates us to carry on a prophetic mission on our daily frontier. I dare say that our educational mission in today's world is a battlefield on the frontier. Faced with the greed generated by a neo-liberal model of life, our service of education cannot stand in any comfort zone or neutral position.

Every day, as a school teacher, I am confronted with unjust policies based on human greed. Recently, the political situation in Korea caused us much suffering and soul-searching, particularly because President Park, who was removed from office through impeachment, is our alumna. The corruption of our government challenges us to reflect on our service of education with fundamental questions: Whom, how and why do we educate? Do we teach our students to be active citizens or just part of a passive mass?

Hannah Arendt maintained that evil comes from the tendency of ordinary people to obey orders and conform to mass opinion without critical evaluation. Such thoughtlessness, I think, is our sin in Korean society, and educators have a great responsibility. If we cannot contribute to a radical reshaping of society, our institutions have no meaning.

To overcome the unjust realities in Korea, we RSCJ are trying to renew our ways of being, ways of teaching, and ways of organizing ourselves. It demands our discerning efforts with analysis, logical reasoning, and critical vision as we are faced with hidden intentions and manipulations of the social and political agenda. It demands our intellectual asceticism. On this battlefield, we hear the voice of Philippine: "Go! Be courageous and be patient!"

Image: Marianne Tavares, RSCJ

Oak Leaves

Marianne Tavares, RSCJ
Province of England-Wales

Philippine's surname, Duchesne, means "of oak." For this reason we have always associated Philippine with the oak tree – the white oak that has leaves with rounded lobes. Another major species is the red oak with leaves with pointed lobes. Last year, the cabin in which I made my retreat was surrounded by white and red oaks. This cabin was also built by an aboriginal man. In this environment, while pondering our 2016 General Chapter Calls, I found myself painting a red oak leaf growing between two white oak leaves.

Philippine sailed from France in a ship across stormy seas in 1818 and landed in New Orleans – a rough journey that took over two months. This French woman who spoke only French crossed many frontiers – geographical, cultural, spiritual, social – in faith, as she responded to God's call.

What might this painting be saying to us? Two white oak leaves supporting the growth of a red oak leaf may be Philippine protecting and blessing us as we explore new and different frontiers, holding our ventures close. New frontiers, today, may be very different from what they were for Philippine. We are invited to be open to listening/hearing as new frontiers beckon. Some of us may be called afar, but new frontiers can also appear just where we are, inviting us to go to new peripheries "to accompany the life that is emerging there, to defend justice, peace and the integrity of creation in response to those who are searching for meaning in their lives, those who have been wounded, displaced, and excluded because of poverty, violence and environmental degradation." In the painting, Saint Philippine Duchesne is saying, "Have courage, have faith." This holy woman, who was known to the Potawatomi as a woman of perpetual prayer, prays with us now as we face and respond to the challenges of our time. ❧

Image: Erika Tornya, RSCJ

It's Never Too Late!

Erika Tornya, RSCJ
Hungary, Province of Central Europe

Our human tendency is to set expectations for ourselves, resisting the creativity of the Holy Spirit within us. We want to know how and when things will take their course. When life does not go as we wish, we believe that God is not really listening to us. Some people think it is too late to explore new ways because they are too old.

Let us imagine what it meant to a forty-eight-year-old woman to leave everything behind. When Philippine entered the Order of the Visitation in Grenoble, France, at the age of eighteen, she could not imagine the French Revolution that would force her to leave only five years later. She waited for nine years to return to her monastic life; and then for three years, she tried to reorganize the order in Grenoble, with little success. Then, at the age of thirty-five, she met Madeleine Sophie Barat, joining her in the Society of the Sacred Heart. This encounter gave her new goals and perspectives. Once again, she was able to leave everything behind. It was not until she was forty-eight-years-old that Philippine sailed to America, responding to her missionary call.

What did Philippine need to take these difficult decisions? Openness, faith, courage, patience, and strong inner freedom. She did not compare herself with others or her contemporaries in terms of how she evaluated her life or what she had achieved in her life so far. Instead, through constant prayer, with persistence in the presence of God, her deep desires were satisfied. The fire of the Heart of Jesus and the love and acceptance of her lived reality gave her strength to endure.

Lord Jesus, create in us inner freedom, space where we can accept our reality with love. Open our hearts to listen to your Spirit, alive in our hearts and in our world. ❧

Image: artist unknown

Poem to Saint Rose Philippine

Kevin Jimenez, student of U. E. Santa Magdalena Sofía
Caracas, Venezuela

Wonderful flower, you who daily nourish the faith and hope of millions of people.

Given a pure and generous soul, incarnated in your infinite goodness
and love for people, such are you, O Saint Rose!

God decided to send you into the world on August 29th, 1769. At the time
of your birth, an old woman who was dying prophesied your birth
as a shooting star passed over.

You gave yourself to caring for prisoners and all who were suffering,
giving them peace, love and joy.

In your moments of prayer and solitude you wrote to our Mother Sophie Barat,
"When you say to me, 'I send you' I shall reply, 'I will go immediately.'" That showed
the depth of your vocation and your courage within the Society of the Sacred Heart.

Sophie Barat, your great friend, said to you, "When shall I know that you have reached
that happy state in which God alone suffices, in which his holy will is the source of
all our actions?"

Your perseverance in your desires is a worthy example not only for the students of this
school, but for all.

Images: Harry Weber and Mimaki Kazuko

Fortitude and Love: Ukon Takayama and Philippine Duchesne

Eriko Oyama, RSCJ
Province of Japan

On the seventh of February, 2017, the Catholic Church of Japan was newly blessed by the beatification of Justo Ukon Takayama (1543-1615). Ukon was a prominent Christian leader of the church in sixteenth century Japan. Reflecting on his life in troubled times, I find similarities between Ukon and Philippine Duchesne, especially in their spirituality of prayer and in their perseverance.

At the age of twelve, Ukon was baptized with his father, Dario, and touched by the powerful message of the Gospel. Ukon first followed his father, but later, he had a conversion experience. Confronted with a critical choice, after discernment, he abandoned worldly success and chose faith. In an age of ambition and armed conflicts, Ukon lost everything by choosing faith. As the anti-Christian edict was issued and persecution began, he became an exile in different places in Japan for twenty-eight years. Yet he persisted in his service to others. His sincerity and mercy as an educator attracted people; communities were naturally formed around him. Eventually, he was forced to leave Japan for his final exile in the Philippines. He reached Manila only to die of a high fever.

Philippine's life was marked by her patience and humility, while Ukon is remembered as a person who "lowered himself." Following Christ who humbled himself, Ukon abandoned worldly success and lived in simplicity. Neither Ukon nor Philippine ever saw any success, but they never abandoned their missionary vocation. In apparent failure, their love and fortitude shone forth. Prayer was their great support.

Living in the unstable world of today, we can learn from a man of the sixteenth century and a woman of the nineteenth century the power of choosing God in trust and faith. ❧

Image: Donna Collins, RSCJ
Province of United States-Canada

What Have We Learned From Her?

T. Gavan Duffy

In 1940, T. Gavan Duffy asked a question about Philippine Duchesne: *What have we learned from her?*

Duffy answered the question himself:

> We have learned . . .
>> the value of a steadfast purpose;
>> the success of failure
>> and the unimportance of our standards of success;
>> the power of grace released by deep, divine desires
>> and simple duty daily done.

Nearing the end of these reflections, we make that question our own:

What have we learned from her? ❧

Sculpture: Gianfranco Tassara of Inspired Artisans
Garden of the Cathedral Basilica of St. Louis
Image: Linda Behrens

Bicentennial Prayer

Composed for the Sacred Heart Family around the world
on the occasion of the 200th Anniversary
of Philippine's arrival in the New World

Spirit of the living God,
you first breathed over the waters of creation,
and one day you breathed a passion
    into the heart of Philippine Duchesne.
You called her to cross the waters to a New World,
to bring the message of your compassion and love
to a land and peoples already dear to your heart.
Not knowing the language of the land,
she spoke the language of the heart –
    of love and prayer,
    of attention and openness,
    of steadfast purpose and living faith.
As the Sacred Heart family around the world,
we are the harvest of the seeds she sowed.
Bless, now, our ever-new world,
with Philippine's spirit of great-hearted courage.
Fill us with her desire to cross frontiers,
especially those furthest from the touch of hope.
Renew the whole Church in its missionary spirit
    and give us Philippine's zeal
    to spread your compassion and love to the ends of the earth.
We ask all this in your name, triune God,
whose love knows no borders or boundaries,
and who sends us to make known that love in the heart of the world
now and forever. Amen. ✿

À la plus grande gloire des sacrés cœurs de Jésus et Marie.

Copie abrégée du journal commencé à St Charles, et continué à St Ferdinand et à St Louis pour la Société du Sacré-Cœur. (Commencé 3 Janvier 1819)

Les premières religieuses du Sacré-Cœur, venues en Amérique sont Mesdames Philippine Duchesne Supérieure, Octavie Berthold assistante, Eugénie Audé admonitrice et les sœurs Marguerite Manteau et Catherine Lamare. Marguerite fut prise à Poitiers, les autres partirent de Paris le 8 février 1818, étant toutes professes. Elles reçurent à leur départ la bénédiction de leur vénérable mère Générale, du vénérable Monsieur Perreau confesseur de la maison et faisant les fonctions de Supérieur général pour Monseigneur de Périgord archevêque de Paris et grand aumônier de France. Le Père Varin auteur des Constitutions de la société, et plusieurs autres Pères Jésuites les bénirent aussi. Elles eurent pour compagnon de voyage jusqu'à Bordeaux Mr Evremont Holstein (depuis prêtre), Madame Vincent supérieure d'une maison religieuse (depuis un an ou deux) [......] Dans sa maison jusqu'à l'embarquement [..............] frère de leur Mère Générale [..................] copié à Monsgr par Dubourg évêque [......................] visité. Elles partirent [...................] de la bénédiction du Saint [...................] avait [.............] samedi, dans la chapelle [...........................] messe ce jour là pour les [...............] Dubourg [.....] Tournier frère et sœur de Monseigneur [..............] les accompagnant jusqu'à la Garonne d'où [................] au vaisseau. Où s'arrête [..........................] cure procura un logement [.......................] vaisseau qui s'appelait [.....] Recca et avait pour capitaine Mr Le Tourneur. Monsieur Martial grand vicaire de Monseigneur Dubourg et Mr Evremont entrèrent avec elles dans le bâtiment le jeudi Saint 19 Mars consacré à St Joseph. Elles éprouvèrent toutes sortes d'égards de la part du capitaine et des passagers. La nourriture était saine et abondante, on les servit en maigre tous les vendredis, elles pouvaient se confesser, communier, avoir la messe les dimanches et dans la semaine quelquefois, quand le tems le permettait.

Timeline of Philippine's Life

August 29, 1769	Birth in Grenoble, France, second oldest of seven girls and one boy
Spring, 1788	Entry into the Visitation monastery of Sainte-Marie d'En-Haut in Grenoble, disbanded in 1792 by the French Revolution
December 1804	Entry into the Society of the Sacred Heart
November 21, 1805	First vows at Sainte-Marie with six companions
December 15, 1815	Election as secretary general of the Society, move to Paris
December 16, 1815	Final vows
February 8, 1818	Departure from Paris for Bordeaux with four companions, bound for America
March 21, 1818	The *Rebecca* set sail
May 29, 1818	Arrival at New Orleans, feast of the Sacred Heart
September 7, 1818	Arrival at St. Charles, Missouri
September 14, 1818	Opening of the first day school west of the Mississippi River
September 3, 1819	Move of the community and school to Florissant on the east side of the Missouri River
August 5, 1821	Departure of Eugénie Audé and Mary Ann Layton to found a school in Grand Coteau, Louisiana
1825	Foundation of the third house at Saint Michael, Louisiana
April 17, 1825	Profession of Mathilde Xavier Hamilton, the first in the Society in America
May 2, 1827	Foundation of the fourth house in south St. Louis, the City House
October 1840	Philippine's relief from the position of superior
June 29, 1841	Departure for the mission to the Potawatomi at Sugar Creek, Kansas
June 19, 1842	Return of Philippine from Sugar Creek to St. Charles
November 16, 1852	Visit of Anna du Rousier, visitator general, to St. Charles
November 18, 1852	Death of Philippine during the noon Angelus
May 12, 1940	Beatification of Philippine by Pope Pius XII
July 3, 1988	Canonization by Pope John Paul II

CPSIA information can be obtained
at www.ICGtesting.com
Printed in the USA
JSHW011743231019
2043JS00002B/4